Cash Under the Mattress

THE ULTIMATE ESTATE AND CRISIS HANDBOOK

By Philip Giroux & Sally Lamb

authorHOUSE®

AuthorHouse™
1663 Liberty Drive
Bloomington, IN 47403
www.authorhouse.com
Phone: 1-800-839-8640

First published by AuthorHouse 10/11/2011

ISBN: 978-1-4567-0110-9 (sc)
ISBN: 978-1-4567-0111-6 (e)

Library of Congress Control Number: 2010917769

Printed in the United States of America
This book is printed on acid-free paper.

Cover Illustration: Sally Lamb
Cover Design: Christopher Harrity
Edited by: Sue McNiel, Patty Gissell, and Nancy Lamb
Computer and Technical Support: Randy Sheldon
Legal Advice: William E. Fields
Back Cover Photographs: Barry Schwartz, Mark Savage
Acknowledgements for their advice and counsel:
George Sarkis, Sam Watters, and Tony Carr

THE FAINTEST INK
IS BETTER THAN
THE STRONGEST
MEMORY

CONFUCIUS
551-479 B.C.

Dedicated to Our Parents

With Special Appreciation to Barbara, Sue and Patty
For all their love and endless hours of help

TABLE OF CONTENTS

Introduction:

Beginning at the Beginning

AN OUNCE OF PREVENTION...

Cash Under The Mattress is a short, simple, and user-friendly handbook to help you plan your own legacy. Pared down to the essentials, this simple, yet effective tool makes planning effortless. Designed to minimize and, in most cases, eliminate unanswered questions, unknown wishes, and possible conflicts between potential beneficiaries. Your loved ones will thank you for your honesty and willingness to take on a serious and challenging subject.

When completed, it is the one book you will want stored with your most important papers, or in your emergency file, or in your safe deposit box. Take it with you on a trip as a reference, should something happen to you while you are away from home.

In *Cash Under the Mattress,* each chapter forms a building block for the pyramid of a life — a beginning, a middle, and an end. This is the beginning of your story — a story only you can tell. The base covers birth and childhood, the middle deals with adult life, and the end confronts old age (may you live so long) and . . . deep breath . . . death.

The greatest benefits this book offers is peace of mind that comes from knowing you have done everything you can to make this process as pain free as possible. That is the gift you give. That is the legacy you leave.

NOTES FROM THE AUTHORS

PHILIP

Imagine you are a pebble tossed into a vast pond. You create ripples throughout your life, affecting not only those close to you, but the world in which you live.

It wasn't easy talking to my parents about creating a Will. Talking about funeral plans wasn't a piece of cake, either. But once we overcame the initial discomfort of dealing with reality, they agreed this task was not only a good idea, it was critical. Otherwise, the primary legacy they'd leave my brother and me would be an unforgettable and indecipherable mess.

Since all of us wanted to avoid that eventuality, we set to work sorting and organizing. Fortunately, my parents had begun the process before I broached the subject. They had already placed their personal instructions in metal boxes — one gold and one silver. In addition to their pre-planning, we decided to write down all their basic information in an easy-to-understand book to help them clarify their wishes. I felt it would help us deal with the aftermath of their loss.

My father and mother died one year apart.

After each of their deaths, I went through the shiny metal boxes containing their instructions regarding bank and pension accounts and their lists of contacts, such as banker, attorney and accountant. They had also included details for giving memorabilia to friends and personal items to charity.

Because of their foresight and their willingness to deal with the reality of their future deaths, I was spared the pain of second-guessing their final wishes. I knew how they wanted their funeral to be conducted, how and where they wanted to be buried, who they wanted to administer their Will, and where their heirlooms were kept.

In spite of all of our advance planning, it was only in the aftermath of their deaths that I realized a lot of critical information had been overlooked. The emotional transition of dealing with death was more layered and demanding than I had anticipated. The array of loopholes and puzzles left behind for me to deal with was staggering.

Shortly after I had finally tied up all the loose ends of their estate, my friend, Sally Lamb, was encountering similar problems.

After the death of Sally's father, we decided to create *Cash Under the Mattress* — a handbook that is thoughtful, friendly, concise and easy-to-use. We wanted a book that invites thought, outlines detail, and creates a clear structure to guide parents and family members through difficult times.

SALLY

When my father died, my two sisters and I were faced with decisions to make and problems to solve that were difficult. Even though our eighty-three year-old mother was there to help, we were overwhelmed with all that needed to be done.

Our parents had been married for sixty years. We assumed that they had taken care of estate matters, and indeed, the legal work had been handled. Planning a funeral and reception in just a few days, however, caught us unprepared.

My mother, of course, did what she could, but the bulk of the work fell to us. All four of us suffered from shock and we were traveling in uncharted territory. We had no map or guidelines to help us through this difficult period. When you're dealing with the death of someone close to you, shock and grief tend to take over, and there is little time to linger with those feelings.

Over the years, of course, we had all been to funerals and receptions, but we had no idea of what was involved to make these events happen. Just gathering information for the obituary, making travel and accommodation plans for friends and relatives, selecting music, writing the eulogy and hosting a large reception was so much to deal with — within a few days. You must react quickly to handle an enormous amount of detailed planning, when all you really want to do is rest.

When our mom died three years later, we were better prepared. We had our previous lists so we knew what needed to be done. And yet, as we plodded down this familiar path, stained by tears and sorrow, we still encountered formidable obstacles.

This time we were now closing down our parents' entire estate. All the legal work was done, but we had to deal with the house, the belongings, and the memorabilia. If our parents had designated who got what and what to do with these things in advance, we could have been spared a lot of anguish, confusion and stress. We were now faced with a new set of problems without any guidance.

Philip and I had already started *Cash Under the Mattress,* and we were sure our similar experiences were not all that uncommon.

We wanted to write a book to help others avoid the problems that we went through. It would also be something we would give to our family and friends. We began to realize that our experiences applied to millions of other people who could be helped by plain solutions to complicated problems.

Our goal is to help others get organized and to minimize the guess work that accompanies a death. We know, first hand, that not knowing what to do, adds unnecessary anxiety, stress, and grief to already painful circumstances. The loss of someone you love is never easy, but there are things you can do — preventative measures you can take — to smooth the path before you. That is why we have written this book.

BEFORE YOU BEGIN

WHY NOW?

When someone dies, heirs gather. Whether it's for monetary, psychological or tangible reasons, your legacy will be discussed and dissected. In the process, conflicts may emerge as possessions are distributed and your estate is settled.

We've all heard the horror stories: family members turn against each other and disagreements and resentments may occur. In the wake of a death, siblings, step parents and children often behave in ways that are, to say the least, unflattering. These dissensions are not easy to confront and defuse. Sometimes as the division of possessions takes place, heirs develop unusual alliances with one another.

This handbook is designed to preempt unpleasant confrontations and prevent the kinds of permanent rifts that happen when siblings, parents and step families need to deal with unresolved estate issues. Whether you are organizing your own estate or you are helping your parents organize theirs, this book offers practical ways to avoid the typical pitfalls families confront when an inheritance — either large or small — is involved. You may think that you do not really own much. But, look around you. Look at all the things you have throughout your home. It all adds up, and it all has to go somewhere.

Your reward for taking the time to face and deal with these personal and legal challenges in advance will provide relief and peace of mind for those involved in your life and your estate. Furthermore, your family members may be relieved of an enormous burden. This book will help in the process of sorting out and simplifying complicated matters.

Once your plans are written down, that tiny voice nagging at the back of your consciousness will no longer ask, "What if something happens and . . .?" Instead, you'll rest easy in the knowledge that your affairs have been settled and, if you have children, that you've done everything you can to ease their conflict and pain.

Of course, confronting the facts of life — as well as death — means that all of you will be forced to discuss subjects that are uncomfortable. But if you work together, disagreements can be confronted and overcome in realistic and constructive ways. For example, you may have to face some uncomfortable issues. For instance, do both siblings want the antique clock or the stamp collection? Should the stocks be divided evenly among the children or should each child receive different investments? This isn't the time to be lulled into a false sense of security. Let's face it. That diamond ring might be pretty now, but it'll turn ugly in an instant when both siblings want it. Don't let it become a potential battle. Designate it now. So many people think that it is best to leave it up to the children to make those decisions. It is actually harder on them. The more effort you make to do advance planning, the fewer problems there will be later.

12 WAYS TO AVOID CONFLICT
<u>BEFORE</u> AND <u>AFTER</u> SOMEONE DIES

Confront the issues of death and dying now.
"Too late" could arrive as soon as tomorrow.

1) Define your desires and share them with your heirs. It is not all about who gets what, but also about your wishes for how you hope your family will come together after you die. If you put these wishes in writing, family members will feel more obliged to behave in honorable ways, thus defusing possible conflicts down the line.

2) Ask each person to make a list of their favorite things in your house — what tangible items they would like to inherit. The items should be listed in order of importance. Compare the priorities and parcel out the items when you are ready.

3) When two or more people want the same thing, draw straws. Those who do not "win" should be allowed to get their next choice on the list.

4) Walk through your house and put name tags on the bottom of items that each person wants and make a list of them to be kept in your safe deposit box.

5) When it comes to dividing an estate, it helps heirs come to peace with your decisions if you tell them how and why you have arrived at particular conclusions.

6) Write a letter of agreement concerning the distribution of items that the heirs can sign in each other's presence.

7) If there are serious issues that cannot be resolved, hire an expert in conflict resolution to help you settle the differences.

8) If you have more than one adult child, give them equal power or responsibility wherever possible: Co-Trustees, Co-Executors, or a Joint Power of Attorney.

9) Make it clear to your heirs that gifting is not etched in stone. Negotiations are not only possible, they are encouraged.

10) Select a neutral territory — a garage, a storage unit — where you can place undesignated items. You can store something here until a decision is made whether to give it to someone, sell it, auction it, or donate it.

11) To put a lid on simmering feuds that could arise between beneficiaries, establish a "cut-off date" at which ill feelings will end. Otherwise, they could spend the rest of their years fretting over what they did not inherit; Set a deadline — both personal and familial — of one to three years, after which an heir must let go of their discontent.

12) Don't forget about your safe deposit box. Those items should be reviewed and listed in your give away pile.

LET'S GET STARTED

There's no time like the present to get started with writing down and preserving all the information that you and your loved ones will need to deal with a crisis. Think about what you want and don't want, then write down the particulars of your life and your personal requests. Although this might feel like a sad task, the truth is that your loved ones will appreciate the opportunity to fulfill your wishes.

Take the time now to make the transition easier for those you hold closest to your heart. This is the way you thank them for all they have meant to you. And this is how you say, "I love you."

CHAPTER ONE

PERSONAL: THE NITTY GRITTY

CHAPTER ONE

PERSONAL:
THE NITTY GRITTY

This chapter involves your basic personal information, those small details that your loved ones may or may not know about you. Here, you list your name, address, licenses, employment and military service as well as various personal items, such as your pets, storage units, and credit card numbers.

One of the realities of life, is the need for passwords for an assortment of private accounts. Because it is secret by nature, usually we do not write it down, but memorize it, and hope we remember it. However, should we become incapacitated, someone will need those passwords. They are the private keys to your digital kingdom.

Note: Perhaps you may want to make a copy of these pages and store the filled in copy in a safe place such as your safe deposit box. We are not liable for you leaving the filled in copy on a park bench.

YOUR NAME, ADDRESS, AND OTHER BASICS

Birth

- Date of Birth _____
- Full Birth Name _____
- Hospital _____
- City _____
- State _____
- Country _____

Full Legal Name

☐ Same
- Full Legal Name _____
- Current Address _____
- City _____ State _____ Zip _____
- Country _____
- Phone _____ Fax _____ Cell _____
- E-mail _____ Other Accounts _____
- Office Phone _____

Citizenship

- Country _____
- U.S. Passport # _____
   ☐ YES
   ☐ NO
- Location _____

Marital Status

☐ Single
☐ Married
☐ Divorced
☐ Widowed

EMPLOYMENT

☐ YES
☐ NO
☐ Self-employed
☐ Employer
☐ Partnership
☐ Corporation

- Business Name _____
- Type of Business (Mfg., Contractor, Sales, etc.) _____
  _____
- Address _____
- City _____ State _____ Zip _____
- Country _____
- Phone _____ Fax _____ Cell _____
- E-mail _____
- Occupation _____
- Date(s) of Service _____
- Branch / Place of Business (if different) _____
- Address _____
- Phone _____ Fax _____ Cell _____
- E-mail _____
- Past Employer(s) and Date(s) of Service _____
  _____
  _____
  _____
  _____
  _____
  _____
  _____
  _____
  _____

MILITARY SERVICE

☐ YES
☐ NO

- Branch
  ☐ Army
  ☐ Marine
  ☐ Navy
  ☐ Air Force
  ☐ Coast Guard
  ☐ Other
- Serial # _____
- Service Dates _____
- Final Rank _____

  _____

- Medal(s) of Distinction _____

  _____
  _____
  _____
  _____
  _____
  _____
  _____
  _____
  _____
  _____
  _____
  _____
  _____
  _____
  _____
  _____
  _____
  _____

CERTIFICATES / LICENSES

☐ Birth Certificate
- Location _____

☐ Marriage License # _____
- Location _____

☐ Passport # _____
- Location _____

☐ Social Security # _____
- Location _____

☐ Driver's License # _____
- Location _____

☐ Auto Registration and License # _____
- Location _____

☐ Plane Registration and License # _____
- Location _____

☐ Motorcycle Registration and License # _____
- Location _____

☐ Boat Registration and License # _____
- Location _____

☐ Professional Licenses and License # _____
- Location _____

☐ Other _____
- Location _____

LOGINS / PASSWORDS

Computer(s):
□ YES

□ NO

□ Desktop

   □ PC   □ Mac   □ Other: _____

Manufacturer/Name: _____

Bios/Encryption/Fingerprint Password(s): _____

Login Name (User name): _____

Password: _____

Password Encrypted Files?

   □ YES

   □ NO

Password: _____

File Name(s)/Location(s): _____

_____

_____

□ Laptop

   □ PC   □ Mac   □ Other: _____

Manufacturer/Name: _____

Bios/Encryption/Fingerprint Password(s): _____

Login Name (User name): _____

Password: _____

Password Encrypted Files?

   □ YES

   □ NO

Password: _____

File Name(s)/Location(s): _____

_____

_____

Domain Names Owned: _____

Registered with: _____

Login: _____

Password: _____

- Security Question 1: _____
- Security Question 1 answer: _____
- Security Question 2: _____
- Security Question 2 answer: _____
- Security Question 3: _____
- Security Question 3 answer: _____

Email:

☐ YES

☐ NO

E-Mail 1:

- E-mail: _____
- Address/URL/Server: _____
- Account type (Pop3/IMAP/Exchange/etc.): _____
- Username (Login Name): _____
- Password: _____

E-Mail 2:

- E-mail: _____
- Address/URL/Server: _____
- Account type (Pop3/IMAP/Exchange/etc.): _____
- Username (Login Name): _____
- Password: _____

E-Mail 3:

- E-mail: _____
- Address/URL/Server: _____
- Account type (Pop3/IMAP/Exchange/etc.): _____
- Username (Login Name): _____
- Password: _____

Online Banking:

☐ YES

☐ NO

Bank 1:

- Bank Address (URL): _____
- Username (Login Name): _____
- Password: _____
- 2nd Authentication (image/etc): _____
- Security Question 1: _____
- Security Question 1 answer: _____
- Security Question 2: _____
- Security Question 2 answer: _____
- Security Question 3: _____
- Security Question 3 answer: _____

Bank 2:

- Bank Address (URL): _____
- Username (Login Name): _____
- Password: _____
- 2nd Authentication (image/etc): _____
- Security Question 1: _____
- Security Question 1 answer: _____
- Security Question 2: _____
- Security Question 2 answer: _____
- Security Question 3: _____
- Security Question 3 answer: _____

Online Brokerage:
- ☐ YES
- ☐ NO

Brokerage 1:
- Brokerage Address (URL): _____
- Username (Login Name): _____
- Password: _____
- 2nd Authentication (image/etc): _____
- Security Question 1: _____
- Security Question 1 answer: _____
- Security Question 2: _____
- Security Question 2 answer: _____
- Security Question 3: _____
- Security Question 3 answer: _____

Brokerage 2:
- Brokerage Address (URL): _____
- Username (Login Name): _____
- Password: _____
- 2nd Authentication (image/etc): _____
- Security Question 1: _____
- Security Question 1 answer: _____
- Security Question 2: _____
- Security Question 2 answer: _____
- Security Question 3: _____
- Security Question 3 answer: _____

Home Security: _____
Primary Home: _____
Password: _____

Notes: _____
_____
_____

ATM / CREDIT CARDS / DEBIT
(Visa, Master Card, American Express, etc.)

☐ YES
☐ NO

- Card Type _____
- Name _____
- Account # _____
- Expiration Date _____
- Location _____
- Password _____
- Annual Fee _____

- Card Type _____
- Name _____
- Account # _____
- Expiration Date _____
- Location _____
- Password _____
- Annual Fee _____

- Card Type _____
- Name _____
- Account # _____
- Expiration Date _____
- Location _____
- Password _____
- Annual Fee _____

- Card Type _____
- Name _____
- Account # _____
- Expiration Date _____
- Location _____
- Password _____
- Annual Fee _____

- Card Type _____
- Name _____
- Account # _____
- Expiration Date _____
- Location _____
- Password _____
- Annual Fee _____

- Card Type _____
- Name _____
- Account # _____
- Expiration Date _____
- Location _____
- Password _____
- Annual Fee _____

AIRLINE FREQUENT FLYER ACCOUNTS

☐ YES
☐ NO

- Airline _____
- Account # _____
- Phone _____
- Password _____

- Airline _____
- Account # _____
- Phone _____
- Password _____

- Airline _____
- Account # _____
- Phone _____
- Password _____

- Airline _____
- Account # _____
- Phone _____
- Password _____

- Airline _____
- Account # _____
- Phone _____
- Password _____

PETS

Dog
- Breed _____
- Name and Age _____
- License # _____
- Vet _____
- Address _____
- Phone _____ Fax _____ Cell _____
- E-mail _____
- Kennel _____
- Trainer _____
- Caretaker _____
- Person or Organization to Adopt My Pet When I Die _____

Dog
- Breed _____
- Name and Age _____
- License # _____
- Vet _____
- Address _____
- Phone _____ Fax _____ Cell _____
- E-mail _____
- Kennel _____
- Trainer _____
- Caretaker _____
- Person or Organization to Adopt My Pet When I Die _____

Cat

- Breed _____
- Name and Age _____
- License # _____
- Vet _____
- Address _____
- Phone _____ Fax _____ Cell _____
- E-mail _____
- Kennel _____
- Trainer _____
- Caretaker _____
- Person or Organization to Adopt My Pet When I Die _____

Cat

- Breed _____
- Name and Age _____
- License # _____
- Vet _____
- Address _____
- Phone _____ Fax _____ Cell _____
- E-mail _____
- Kennel _____
- Trainer _____
- Caretaker _____
- Person or Organization to Adopt My Pet When I Die _____

Other

- Breed _____
- Name and Age _____
- License # _____
- Vet _____
- Address _____
- Phone _____ Fax _____ Cell _____
- E-mail _____
- Kennel _____
- Trainer _____
- Caretaker _____
- Person or Organization to Adopt My Pet When I Die _____

Other

- Breed _____
- Name and Age _____
- License # _____
- Vet _____
- Address _____
- Phone _____ Fax _____ Cell _____
- E-mail _____
- Kennel _____
- Trainer _____
- Caretaker _____
- Person or Organization to Adopt My Pet When I Die _____

CHAPTER TWO

FAMILY:
YOUR INNER CIRCLE

CHAPTER TWO

FAMILY:
YOUR INNER CIRCLE

In this chapter you can record the names of your family and those closest to you. It is also your opportunity to designate the individuals to carry out your last wishes.

You might consider including a family tree and spending some time labeling photographs. No one will remember who's who down the road.

Also, we strongly recommend that you assemble a list of those people you wish to be notified when you die. This includes family and friends scattered across the world, as well as your business associates.

If you wish, you can even compose the letter you want to be sent to them. You can be serious, of course. But this is also your chance to have fun and to express your gratitude to all the people in your life who have touched you in one way or another. Making your exit with a thank you is not a bad way to go.

FAMILY DIRECTORY

Spouse / Significant Other _____

- Name _____
- Address _____
- City _____
- State _____
- Country _____
- Phone _____ Fax _____ Cell _____
- E-mail _____
- Deceased
    - ☐ YES
    - ☐ NO

Former Spouse / Significant Other _____

- Name _____
- Address _____
- City _____
- State _____
- Country _____
- Phone _____ Fax _____ Cell _____
- E-mail _____
- Deceased
    - ☐ YES
    - ☐ NO

- ## Son(s)
Name, Address, City, State, Country, Phone, Fax, Cell, E-mail

_____

_____

_____

_____

_____

_____

_____

_____

- ## Daughter(s)
Name, Address, City, State, Country, Phone, Fax, Cell, E-mail

_____

_____

_____

_____

_____

_____

_____

_____

- ## Mother
Name, Address, City, State, Country, Phone, Fax, Cell, E-mail

_____

_____

_____

_____

- **Father**

Name, Address, City, State, Country, Phone, Fax, Cell, E-mail

_____

_____

_____

_____

_____

- **Brother(s)**

Name, Address, City, State, Country, Phone, Fax, Cell, E-mail

_____

_____

_____

_____

_____

_____

_____

_____

_____

- **Sister(s)**

Name, Address, City, State, Country, Phone, Fax, Cell, E-mail

_____

_____

_____

_____

_____

_____

_____

_____

_____

- **Aunt(s)**

Name, Address, City, State, Country, Phone, Fax, Cell, E-mail

_____

_____

_____

_____

_____

_____

_____

_____

_____

- **Uncle(s)**

Name, Address, City, State, Country, Phone, Fax, Cell, E-mail

_____

_____

_____

_____

_____

_____

_____

_____

_____

_____

- **Stepmother**

Name, Address, City, State, Country, Phone, Fax, Cell, E-mail

_____

_____

_____

_____

_____

- **Stepfather**
Name, Address, City, State, Country, Phone, Fax, Cell, E-mail

_____

_____

_____

_____

_____

- **Mother-in-law**
Name, Address, City, State, Country, Phone, Fax, Cell, E-mail

_____

_____

_____

_____

_____

- **Father-in-law**
Name, Address, City, State, Country, Phone, Fax, Cell, E-mail

_____

_____

_____

_____

_____

- ## Grandmother
Name, Address, City, State, Country, Phone, Fax, Cell, E-mail

_____

_____

_____

_____

_____

- ## Grandfather
Name, Address, City, State, Country, Phone, Fax, Cell, E-mail

_____

_____

_____

_____

_____

- ## Grandchildren
Name, Address, City, State, Country, Phone, Fax, Cell, E-mail

_____

_____

_____

_____

_____

_____

_____

_____

_____

_____

_____

_____

_____

• **Great Grandchildren, Cousins, Nephews, and Nieces**
Name, Address, City, State, Country, Phone, Fax, Cell, E-mail

_____

_____

_____

_____

_____

_____

_____

_____

_____

_____

_____

_____

_____

_____

_____

_____

_____

_____

_____

_____

_____

_____

_____

_____

_____

_____

_____

_____

_____

_____

_____

_____

FAMILY TREE

Here is a sample family tree for yourself and your children.

For a more complex family tree, visit the many websites that offer more in-depth options, such as, ancestry.com

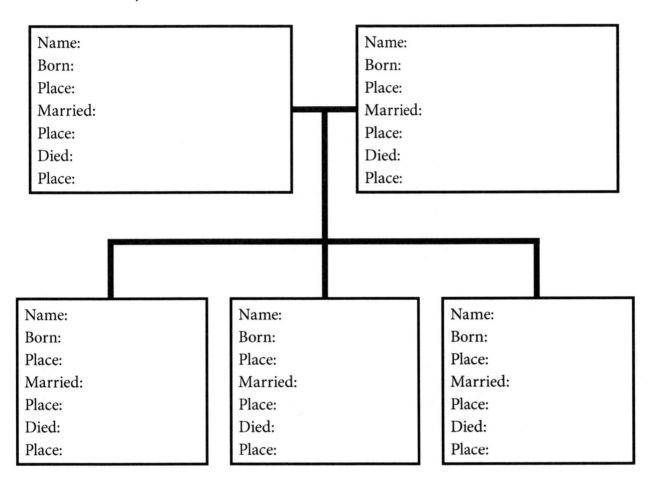

Name:
Born:
Place:
Married:
Place:
Died:
Place:

Name:
Born:
Place:
Married:
Place:
Died:
Place:

Name:
Born:
Place:
Married:
Place:
Died:
Place:

Name:
Born:
Place:
Married:
Place:
Died:
Place:

Name:
Born:
Place:
Married:
Place:
Died:
Place:

CHAPTER THREE

PROPERTY:
WHERE'S ALL YOUR "STUFF"?

Chapter Three

Property:
Where's All Your "Stuff"?

This is where you list all your property — residential, commercial, recreational, and personal possessions — and any donations you wish to make.

By the time you die, chances are you will have accumulated a lot of stuff — big stuff and little stuff, fancy stuff and plain stuff. Unless you have moved recently, or have had the fortitude, courage, or desire to clear out your excess belongings from the attic, basement, closets, or garage, you probably have items taking up every nook and cranny of your home.

Remember that every item you own will have to go into someone else's nook and cranny. So, this is also your chance to clean out and give away any item that you and your family don't want.

If particular items have some "real" value or are meaningful to your family history, be sure to write it down; otherwise the history and memories will be lost. Don't assume that your often-told stories will be remembered accurately. A family heirloom wears many hats: financial, emotional, historical and personal. A mantle clock displayed in your home for thirty years fits into all these categories.

Take advantage of this opportunity before it's too late. Let your heirs know how you want your possessions to be distributed. Make it your choice to designate or donate. It is also okay to surprise your family and friends by labeling items with their names, and having these items discovered after you die.

Be sure to review what is in your safe deposit box as well. Update your Will or Trust and your list regularly, editing your distributions as you see fit.

Whatever strategy you decide to use, write it down and do it now.

RESIDENTIAL

Primary Home
- ☐ House
- ☐ Condo
- ☐ Apartment

- ☐ Own
- ☐ Rent / Lease

Own (Primary Home)
- ☐ YES
- ☐ NO
- Owner(s) _____
- Address _____
- City _____ State _____ Zip _____
- Phone _____ Fax _____ Cell _____
- E-mail _____
- Deed of Trust Title _____
- Location of Deed of Trust _____
- Homeowner's Association
- ☐ YES
- ☐ NO
    - Dues $ _____
    - Association Name _____
    - Management Company _____
    - Phone _____
    - Address _____

Rent / Lease (Primary Home)

☐ YES

☐ NO

- Owner(s) _____
- Address _____
- City _____ State _____ Zip _____
- Contact Person _____
- Phone _____ Fax _____ Cell _____
- E-mail _____
- Monthly Rent $ _____
- Terms _____
- Location of Rental / Lease Agreement _____
- Buy Out Agreement with Owner

    ☐ YES / Location _____

    ☐ NO

- Homeowner's Association

    ☐ YES

    ☐ NO

    Dues $ _____

    Association Name _____

    Management Company _____

    Phone _____

    Address _____

Mortgage / Lender (Primary Home)

☐ YES

☐ NO

- Company _____
- Address _____
- City _____ State _____ Zip _____
- Contact Person _____
- Phone _____ Fax _____ Cell _____
- E-mail _____
- Account # _____
- Account Title _____

Second Mortgage / Lender (Primary Home)

☐ YES

☐ NO

- Company _____
- Address _____
- City _____ State _____ Zip _____
- Contact Person _____
- Phone _____ Fax _____ Cell _____
- E-mail _____
- Account # _____
- Account Title _____

Equity Line (Primary Home)
- ☐ YES
- ☐ NO

- Company _____
- Address _____
- City _____ State _____ Zip _____
- Contact Person _____
- Phone _____ Fax _____ Cell _____
- E-mail _____
- Account # _____
- Account Title _____

Home Security Company (Primary Home)
- ☐ YES
- ☐ NO

- Company _____
- Address _____
- City _____ State _____ Zip _____
- Contact Person _____
- Phone _____ Fax _____ Cell _____
- Account # _____

Maintenance / Repair Company (Primary Home)

☐ YES

☐ NO

- Name _____
- Address _____
- City _____ State _____ Zip _____
- Contact Person _____
- Phone _____ Fax _____ Cell _____
- Account # _____

Notes (Primary Home)

_____
_____
_____
_____
_____
_____
_____
_____
_____
_____
_____
_____
_____
_____
_____
_____
_____
_____
_____
_____
_____
_____
_____

Second Home
- ☐ House
- ☐ Condo
- ☐ Apartment

- ☐ Own
- ☐ Rent / Lease

- ☐ Rental Property – Please List in "Rentals" Section Below

Own (Second Home)
- ☐ YES
- ☐ NO
- Owner(s) _____
- Address _____
- City _____ State _____ Zip _____
- Phone _____ Fax _____ Cell _____
- E-mail _____
- Deed of Trust Title _____
- Location of Deed of Trust _____
- Homeowner's Association
- ☐ YES
- ☐ NO
  - Dues $ _____
  - Association Name _____
  - Management Company _____
  - Phone _____
  - Address _____

Rent / Lease (Second Home)

- ☐ YES
- ☐ NO
- Owner(s) _____
- Address _____
- City _____ State _____ Zip _____
- Contact Person _____
- Phone _____ Fax _____ Cell _____
- E-mail _____
- Monthly Rent $_____
- Terms _____
- Location of Rental / Lease Agreement _____
- Buy Out Agreement with Owner
  - ☐ YES / Location _____
  - ☐ NO
- Homeowner's Association
  - ☐ YES
  - ☐ NO
    - Dues $ _____
    - Association Name _____
    - Management Company _____
    - Phone _____
    - Address _____

Mortgage / Lender (Second Home)

☐ YES

☐ NO

- Company _____
- Address _____
- City _____ State _____ Zip _____
- Contact Person _____
- Phone _____ Fax _____ Cell _____
- E-mail _____
- Account # _____
- Account Title _____

Second Mortgage / Lender (Second Home)

☐ YES

☐ NO

- Company _____
- Address _____
- City _____ State _____ Zip _____
- Contact Person _____
- Phone _____ Fax _____ Cell _____
- E-mail _____
- Account # _____
- Account Title _____

Equity Line (Second Home)

☐ YES

☐ NO

- Company _____
- Address _____
- City _____ State _____ Zip _____
- Contact Person _____
- Phone _____ Fax _____ Cell _____
- E-mail _____
- Account # _____
- Account Title _____

Home Security Company (Second Home)

☐ YES

☐ NO

- Company _____
- Address _____
- City _____ State _____ Zip _____
- Contact Person _____
- Phone _____ Fax _____ Cell _____
- Account # _____

Maintenance / Repair Company (Second Home)

☐ YES

☐ NO

- Name _____
- Address _____
- City _____ State _____ Zip _____
- Contact Person _____
- Phone _____ Fax _____ Cell _____
- Account # _____

Notes (Second Home)

_____
_____
_____
_____
_____
_____
_____
_____
_____
_____
_____
_____
_____
_____
_____
_____
_____
_____
_____
_____
_____
_____
_____
_____

RENTALS

Rental #1
- ☐ House
- ☐ Condo
- ☐ Apartment
- Property Address _____
- City _____ State _____ Zip _____
- Owner(s) _____
- Address _____
- City _____ State _____ Zip _____
- Phone _____ Fax _____ Cell _____
- E-mail _____
- Deed of Trust Title _____
- Location of Deed of Trust _____

Rental Property Management Company (Rental #1)
- ☐ YES
- ☐ NO
- Monthly Fee $_____
- Management Company _____
- Contact Person _____
- Address _____
- City _____ State _____ Zip _____
- Phone _____ Fax _____ Cell _____
- E-mail _____

Renter(s) / Lessee(s) (Rental #1)

- Name(s) _____
- Address _____
- City _____ State _____ Zip _____
- Phone _____ Fax _____ Cell _____
- E-mail _____
- Monthly Rent $_____
- Terms _____
- Location of Rental / Lease Agreement_____
- Buy Out Agreement(s) with Owner
  - ☐ YES / Location _____
  - ☐ NO

Homeowner's Association (Rental #1)

- ☐ YES
- ☐ NO
- Association Name _____
- Management Company _____
- Address _____
- City _____ State _____ Zip _____
- Contact Person _____
- Phone _____ Fax _____ Cell _____
- E-mail _____
- Dues $_____
  - ☐ Paid by Owner
  - ☐ Paid by Renter(s) / Lessee(s)

Mortgage / Lender (Rental #1)

    ☐ YES

    ☐ NO

- Company _____
- Address _____
- City _____ State _____ Zip _____
- Contact Person _____
- Phone _____ Fax _____ Cell _____
- E-mail _____
- Account # _____
- Account Title _____

Second Mortgage / Lender (Rental #1)

    ☐ YES

    ☐ NO

- Company _____
- Address _____
- City _____ State _____ Zip _____
- Contact Person _____
- Phone _____ Fax _____ Cell _____
- E-mail _____
- Account # _____
- Account Title _____

Equity Line (Rental #1)

☐ YES

☐ NO

- Company _____
- Address _____
- City _____ State _____ Zip _____
- Contact Person _____
- Phone _____ Fax _____ Cell _____
- E-mail _____
- Account # _____
- Account Title _____

Home Security Company (Rental #1)

☐ YES

☐ NO

- Company _____
- Address _____
- City _____ State _____ Zip _____
- Contact Person _____
- Phone _____ Fax _____ Cell _____
- Account # _____
- Password _____

Maintenance / Repair Company (Rental #1)

☐ YES

☐ NO

- Company _____
- Address _____
- City _____ State _____ Zip _____
- Contact Person _____
- Phone _____ Fax _____ Cell _____
- Account # _____
- Password _____

Notes (Second Home)

_____
_____
_____
_____
_____
_____
_____
_____
_____
_____
_____
_____
_____
_____
_____
_____
_____
_____
_____
_____
_____
_____

Rental #2
- ☐ House
- ☐ Condo
- ☐ Apartment

- Property Address _____
- City _____ State _____ Zip _____
- Owner(s) _____
- Address _____
- City _____ State _____ Zip _____
- Phone _____ Fax _____ Cell _____
- E-mail _____
- Deed of Trust Title _____
- Location of Deed of Trust _____

Rental Property Management Company (Rental #2)
- ☐ YES
- ☐ NO
- Monthly Fee $_____
- Management Company _____
- Contact Person _____
- Address _____
- City _____ State _____ Zip _____
- Phone _____ Fax _____ Cell _____
- E-mail _____

Renter(s) / Lessee(s) (Rental #2)

- Name(s) _____
- Address _____
- City _____ State _____ Zip _____
- Phone _____ Fax _____ Cell _____
- E-mail _____
- Monthly Rent $_____
- Terms _____
- Location of Rental/Lease Agreement_____
- Buy Out Agreement(s) with Owner
  - ☐ YES / Location _____
  - ☐ NO

Homeowner's Association (Rental #2)

  - ☐ YES
  - ☐ NO
- Association Name _____
- Management Company _____
- Address _____
- City _____ State _____ Zip _____
- Contact Person _____
- Phone _____ Fax _____ Cell _____
- E-mail _____
- Dues $_____
  - ☐ Paid by Owner
  - ☐ Paid by Renter(s)/Lessee(s)

Mortgage / Lender (Rental #2)

- ☐ YES
- ☐ NO
- Company _____
- Address _____
- City _____ State _____ Zip _____
- Contact Person _____
- Phone _____ Fax _____ Cell _____
- E-mail _____
- Account # _____
- Account Title _____

Second Mortgage / Lender (Rental #2)

- ☐ YES
- ☐ NO
- Company _____
- Address _____
- City _____ State _____ Zip _____
- Contact Person _____
- Phone _____ Fax _____ Cell _____
- E-mail _____
- Account # _____
- Account Title _____

Equity Line (Rental #2)

- ☐ YES
- ☐ NO
- Company _____
- Address _____
- City _____ State _____ Zip _____
- Contact Person _____
- Phone _____ Fax _____ Cell _____
- E-mail _____
- Account # _____
- Account Title _____

Home Security Company (Rental #2)

- ☐ YES
- ☐ NO
- Company _____
- Address _____
- City _____ State _____ Zip _____
- Contact Person _____
- Phone _____ Fax _____ Cell _____
- Account # _____
- Password _____

Maintenance / Repair Company (Rental #2)

   ☐ YES

   ☐ NO

- Company _____
- Address _____
- City _____ State _____ Zip _____
- Contact Person _____
- Phone _____ Fax _____ Cell _____
- Account # _____
- Password _____

Additional Rental Properties

   ☐ YES

   ☐ NO

_____

_____

_____

_____

_____

_____

_____

_____

_____

_____

_____

_____

_____

_____

_____

_____

_____

_____

_____

COMMERCIAL

☐ YES
☐ NO

- Property Address _____
- Property Type _____
- City _____ State _____ Zip _____
- Owner(s) _____
- Address _____
- City _____ State _____ Zip _____
- Phone _____ Fax _____ Cell _____
- E-mail _____
- Deed of Trust Title _____
- Location of Deed of Trust _____

Tenant Name(s) / Phone (Commercial)

- Tenant #1 _____
- Tenant #2 _____
- Tenant #3 _____
- Tenant #4 _____
- Tenant #5 _____
- Tenant #6 _____
- Tenant #7 _____
- Location of Tenant Agreement(s) _____

Commercial Property Management Company
- ☐ YES
- ☐ NO
- Monthly Fee $_____
- Management Company _____
- Contact Person _____
- Address _____
- City _____ State _____ Zip _____
- Phone _____ Fax _____ Cell _____
- E-mail _____

Mortgage / Lender (Commercial)
- ☐ YES
- ☐ NO
- Company _____
- Address _____
- City _____ State _____ Zip _____
- Contact Person _____
- Phone _____ Fax _____ Cell _____
- E-mail _____
- Account # _____
- Account Title _____

Second Mortgage / Lender (Commercial)

☐ YES

☐ NO

- Company _____
- Address _____
- City _____ State _____ Zip _____
- Contact Person _____
- Phone _____ Fax _____ Cell _____
- E-mail _____
- Account # _____
- Account Title _____

Equity Line (Commercial)

☐ YES

☐ NO

- Company _____
- Address _____
- City _____ State _____ Zip _____
- Contact Person _____
- Phone _____ Fax _____ Cell _____
- E-mail _____
- Account # _____
- Account Title _____

Security Company (Commercial)

☐ YES
☐ NO

- Company _____
- Address _____
- City _____ State _____ Zip _____
- Contact Person _____
- Phone _____ Fax _____ Cell _____
- Account # _____
- Password _____

Maintenance / Repair Company (Commercial)

☐ YES
☐ NO

- Company _____
- Address _____
- City _____ State _____ Zip _____
- Contact Person _____
- Phone _____ Fax _____ Cell _____
- Account # _____
- Password _____

Additional Commercial Properties

☐ YES
☐ NO

_____
_____
_____
_____
_____
_____
_____
_____
_____

STORAGE UNITS

Mini-Storage Unit
    ☐ YES
    ☐ NO
- Location _____
- Name of Storage _____
- Address _____
- Phone _____
- Unit # _____
- Key / Location _____
- Contract # / Location _____
- Monthly Fee $ _____

Personal Safe
    ☐ YES
    ☐ NO
- Location _____
- Combination _____
- Key / Location _____

Safe Deposit Box (also listed in Chapter Four in "Banking" section)
    ☐ YES
    ☐ NO
- Safe Deposit Box # _____
- Bank / Branch _____
- Location of Key _____
- Signature(s) Required _____

AUTO, MOTORCYCLE, BOAT, RV, PLANE

Auto

☐ YES

☐ NO

- Owner(s) _____
- Address _____
- City _____ State _____ Zip _____
- Make _____
- Model/Year _____
- VIN # _____
- License # _____

Location of Auto

- Address _____
- City _____ State _____ Zip _____
- Contact Person _____
- Phone _____ Fax _____ Cell _____
- E-mail _____

Title and Registration of Auto

- ☐ YES
- ☐ NO

- Owner(s) _____
- Address _____
- City _____ State _____ Zip _____
- Contact Person _____
- Phone _____ Fax _____ Cell _____
- E-mail _____

Lender of Auto

- ☐ YES
- ☐ NO

- Company _____
- Account # _____
- Address _____
- City _____ State _____ Zip _____
- Contact Person _____
- Phone _____ Fax _____ Cell _____
- E-mail _____

Motorcycle

☐ YES

☐ NO

- Owner(s) _____
- Address _____
- City _____ State _____ Zip _____
- Make _____
- Model/Year _____
- VIN # _____
- License # _____

Location of Motorcycle

- Address _____
- City _____ State _____ Zip _____
- Contact Person _____
- Phone _____ Fax _____ Cell _____
- E-mail _____

Title and Registration of Motorcycle

- ☐ YES
- ☐ NO
- Owner(s) _____
- Address _____
- City _____ State _____ Zip _____
- Contact Person _____
- Phone _____ Fax _____ Cell _____
- E-mail _____

Lender of Motorcycle

- ☐ YES
- ☐ NO
- Company _____
- Account # _____
- Address _____
- City _____ State _____ Zip _____
- Contact Person _____
- Phone _____ Fax _____ Cell _____
- E-mail _____

Boat

☐ YES

☐ NO

- Owner(s) _____
- Address _____
- City _____ State _____ Zip _____
- Make _____
- Model/Year _____
- VIN # _____
- License # _____

Location of Boat

- Address _____
- City _____ State _____ Zip _____
- Contact Person _____
- Phone _____ Fax _____ Cell _____
- E-mail _____

Title and Registration of Boat

☐ YES

☐ NO

- Owner(s) _____
- Address _____
- City _____ State _____ Zip _____
- Contact Person _____
- Phone _____ Fax _____ Cell _____
- E-mail _____

Lender of Boat

☐ YES

☐ NO

- Company _____
- Account # _____
- Address _____
- City _____ State _____ Zip _____
- Contact Person _____
- Phone _____ Fax _____ Cell _____
- E-mail _____

RV

    ☐ YES

    ☐ NO

- Owner(s) _____
- Address _____
- City _____ State _____ Zip _____
- Make _____
- Model/Year _____
- VIN # _____
- License # _____

Location of RV

- Address _____
- City _____ State _____ Zip _____
- Contact Person _____
- Phone _____ Fax _____ Cell _____
- E-mail _____

Title and Registration of RV

- ☐ YES
- ☐ NO

- Owner(s) _____
- Address _____
- City _____ State _____ Zip _____
- Contact Person _____
- Phone _____ Fax _____ Cell _____
- E-mail _____

Lender of RV

- ☐ YES
- ☐ NO

- Company _____
- Account # _____
- Address _____
- City _____ State _____ Zip _____
- Contact Person _____
- Phone _____ Fax _____ Cell _____
- E-mail _____

Plane

- ☐ YES
- ☐ NO
- Owner(s) _____
- Address _____
- City _____ State _____ Zip _____
- Make _____
- Model/Year _____
- VIN # _____
- License # _____

Location of Plane

- Address _____
- City _____ State _____ Zip _____
- Contact Person _____
- Phone _____ Fax _____ Cell _____
- E-mail _____

Title and Registration of Plane

- ☐ YES
- ☐ NO
- Owner(s) _____
- Address _____
- City _____ State _____ Zip _____
- Contact Person _____
- Phone _____ Fax _____ Cell _____
- E-mail _____

Lender of Plane

- ☐ YES
- ☐ NO
- Company _____
- Account # _____
- Address _____
- City _____ State _____ Zip _____
- Contact Person _____
- Phone _____ Fax _____ Cell _____
- E-mail _____

Miscellaneous – Vehicle(s)

☐ YES

☐ NO

- Owner(s) _____
- Address _____
- City _____ State _____ Zip _____
- Make _____
- Model/Year _____
- VIN # _____
- License # _____

Location of Other Vehicle(s)

- Address _____
- City _____ State _____ Zip _____
- Contact Person _____
- Phone _____ Fax _____ Cell _____
- E-mail _____

Philip Giroux & Sally Lamb

Title and Registration of Vehicle(s)

☐ YES
☐ NO

- Owner(s) _____
- Address _____
- City _____ State _____ Zip _____
- Contact Person _____
- Phone _____ Fax _____ Cell _____
- E-mail _____

Lender of Vehicle(s)

☐ YES
☐ NO

- Company _____
- Account # _____
- Address _____
- City _____ State _____ Zip _____
- Contact Person _____
- Phone _____ Fax _____ Cell _____
- E-mail _____

MORE COLLECTIBLES, JEWELRY, AND OTHER TREASURES
(Include Description and Location)

☐ Art

_____

_____

_____

☐ Furniture

_____

_____

_____

☐ Coins

_____

_____

_____

☐ Photography

_____

_____

_____

☐ Stamps

_____

_____

_____

☐ Jewelry

_____

_____

_____

☐ Books

_____

_____

_____

☐ Other

_____

_____

_____

BELONGINGS – DONATIONS OR GIFTS

Clothing, Jewelry, Furniture, Tools, Collections, etc.

Item #1 _____
- ☐ Gift to Family or Friend
- ☐ Donate to Charity or Organization
- Name of Person / Charity _____
- Address _____
- Phone _____ Fax _____ Cell _____
- E-mail _____

Item #2 _____
- ☐ Gift to Family or Friend
- ☐ Donate to Charity or Organization
- Name of Person / Charity _____
- Address _____
- Phone _____ Fax _____ Cell _____
- E-mail _____

Item #3 _____
- ☐ Gift to Family or Friend
- ☐ Donate to Charity or Organization
- Name of Person / Charity _____
- Address _____
- Phone _____ Fax _____ Cell _____
- E-mail _____

Item #4 _____

   ☐ Gift to Family or Friend
   ☐ Donate to Charity or Organization
- Name of Person / Charity _____
- Address _____
- Phone _____ Fax _____ Cell _____
- E-mail _____

Item #5 _____

   ☐ Gift to Family or Friend
   ☐ Donate to Charity or Organization
- Name of Person / Charity _____
- Address _____
- Phone _____ Fax _____ Cell _____
- E-mail _____

Item #6 _____

   ☐ Gift to Family or Friend
   ☐ Donate to Charity or Organization
- Name of Person / Charity _____
- Address _____
- Phone _____ Fax _____ Cell _____
- E-mail _____

Item #7 _____

    ☐ Gift to Family or Friend

    ☐ Donate to Charity or Organization

- Name of Person / Charity _____
- Address _____
- Phone _____ Fax _____ Cell _____
- E-mail _____

Item #8 _____

    ☐ Gift to Family or Friend

    ☐ Donate to Charity or Organization

- Name of Person / Charity _____
- Address _____
- Phone _____ Fax _____ Cell _____
- E-mail _____

Item #9 _____

    ☐ Gift to Family or Friend

    ☐ Donate to Charity or Organization

- Name of Person / Charity _____
- Address _____
- Phone _____ Fax _____ Cell _____
- E-mail _____

A STORY OF FAMILY HISTORY AND SPECIAL ITEMS

_____
_____
_____
_____
_____
_____
_____
_____
_____
_____
_____
_____
_____
_____
_____
_____
_____
_____
_____
_____
_____
_____
_____
_____
_____
_____
_____
_____
_____
_____

BUSINESS &
FINANCIAL AFFAIRS:
PURSE STRINGS & OTHER THINGS

CHAPTER FOUR

BUSINESS & FINANCIAL AFFAIRS: PURSE STRINGS & OTHER THINGS

This is the list of "who's who" in your financial world. It includes your personal and business information, from where you bank, to who does your taxes, whether you have any pension / retirement plans, such as an IRA or 401 account, to which, if any, credit union you use.

It is important to clearly list the names of the businesses and professionals that you contact. Your heirs need to know, in order to carry out your last wishes.

BANKING

Banks (Local)

- ☐ YES
- ☐ NO

- Bank _____
- Address _____
- City _____ State _____ Zip _____
- Branch _____
- Contact Person _____
- Phone _____ Fax _____ Cell _____
- E-mail _____
- Account #1
  - ☐ Checking
  - ☐ Savings
  - ☐ Joint
  - ☐ Single
  - Account # _____
  - Account Title _____
- Account #2
  - ☐ Checking
  - ☐ Savings
  - ☐ Joint
  - ☐ Single
  - Account # _____
  - Account Title _____

- Account #3
  - ☐ Checking
  - ☐ Savings
  - ☐ Joint
  - ☐ Single
  - Account # _____
  - Account Title _____
- Account #4
  - ☐ Checking
  - ☐ Savings
  - ☐ Joint
  - ☐ Single
  - Account # _____
  - Account Title _____
- Safe Deposit Box # _____
- Location of Key _____
- Signature(s) Required _____

Banks (Out-of-State / Country)

☐ YES

☐ NO

- Bank _____
- Address _____
- City _____ State _____ Zip _____
- Branch _____
- Contact Person _____
- Phone _____ Fax _____ Cell _____
- E-mail _____
- Account #1

  ☐ Checking

  ☐ Savings

  ☐ Joint

  ☐ Single

  Account # _____

  Account Title _____
- Account #2

  ☐ Checking

  ☐ Savings

  ☐ Joint

  ☐ Single

  Account # _____

  Account Title _____

- Account #3
  - ☐ Checking
  - ☐ Savings
  - ☐ Joint
  - ☐ Single
  - Account # _____
  - Account Title _____
- Account #4
  - ☐ Checking
  - ☐ Savings
  - ☐ Joint
  - ☐ Single
  - Account # _____
  - Account Title _____
- Safe Deposit Box # _____
- Location of Key _____
- Signature(s) Required _____

CREDIT UNIONS

☐ YES
☐ NO

- Name of Credit Union _____
- Address _____
- City _____ State _____ Zip _____
- Primary Owner _____
- Address _____
- City _____ State _____ Zip _____
- SS # _____
- Phone _____ Fax _____ Cell _____
- E-mail _____
- Member # _____
- Driver's License # _____
- Savings Account # _____
- Checking Account # _____
- Loan Account # _____
- Mortgage Account # _____
- Equity Line Account # _____
- Membership Fee $ _____
- Employer _____
- Employer Address _____
- City _____ State _____ Zip _____
- Phone _____ Fax _____ Cell _____
- E-mail _____
- Mother's Maiden Name _____

- Joint Owner _____
- Address _____
- City _____ State _____ Zip _____
- Phone _____ Fax _____ Cell _____
- E-mail _____
- SS # _____

(Website address for further SS # information www.ssa.gov)

ACCOUNTANT

☐ YES
☐ NO

- Name of Accountant _____
- Name of Firm _____
- Address _____
- City _____ State _____ Zip _____
- Contact Person _____
- Phone _____ Fax _____ Cell _____
- E-mail _____

TAX PREPARER

Current

- Name of Firm _____
- Address _____
- City _____ State _____ Zip _____
- Contact Person _____
- Phone _____ Fax _____ Cell _____
- E-mail _____

Prior Tax Returns

- Name of Firm _____
- Address _____
- City _____ State _____ Zip _____
- Contact Person _____
- Phone _____ Fax _____ Cell _____
- E-mail _____

PENSIONS / RETIREMENT PLANS

IRA (Individual Retirement Account)
☐ YES
☐ NO

- Name of Firm _____
- Address _____
- City _____ State _____ Zip _____
- Contact Person _____
- Phone _____ Fax _____ Cell _____
- E-mail _____
- Account # _____

- Name of Firm _____
- Address _____
- City _____ State _____ Zip _____
- Contact Person _____
- Phone _____ Fax _____ Cell _____
- E-mail _____
- Account # _____

ROTH IRA

☐ YES

☐ NO

- Name of Firm _____
- Address _____
- City _____ State _____ Zip _____
- Contact Person _____
- Phone _____ Fax _____ Cell _____
- E-mail _____
- Account # _____

KEOGH Plan

☐ YES

☐ NO

- Name of Firm _____
- Address _____
- City _____ State _____ Zip _____
- Contact Person _____
- Phone _____ Fax _____ Cell _____
- E-mail _____
- Account # _____

401 K-Plan
  - ☐ YES
  - ☐ NO

- Name of Firm _____
- Address _____
- City _____ State _____ Zip _____
- Contact Person _____
- Phone _____ Fax _____ Cell _____
- E-mail _____
- Account # _____

SEP IRA
  - ☐ YES
  - ☐ NO

- Name of Firm _____
- Address _____
- City _____ State _____ Zip _____
- Contact Person _____
- Phone _____ Fax _____ Cell _____
- E-mail _____
- Account # _____

ANNUITIES

Annuity #1
□ YES

□ NO

- Type
  - □ Fixed
  - □ Variable
  - □ Other _____
- Owner of Annuity _____
- Name of Insurer _____
- Place of Purchase _____
- Name of Agent _____
- Address _____
- City _____ State _____ Zip _____
- Phone _____ Fax _____ Cell _____
- E-mail _____
- Contract # _____
- Value (approximately) _____
- Beneficiary (Name, Address, Phone(s), Fax, Cell, E-mail)

  Beneficiary #1 _____

  Beneficiary #2 _____

  Beneficiary #3 _____

  Beneficiary #4 _____

Annuity #2

☐ YES

☐ NO

- Type

  ☐ Fixed

  ☐ Variable

  ☐ Other _____

- Owner of Annuity _____
- Name of Insurer _____
- Place of Purchase _____
- Name of Agent _____
- Address _____
- City _____ State _____ Zip _____
- Phone _____ Fax _____ Cell _____
- E-mail _____
- Contract # _____
- Value (approximately) _____
- Beneficiary (Name, Address, Phone(s), Fax, Cell, E-mail)

  Beneficiary #1 _____

  Beneficiary #2 _____

  Beneficiary #3 _____

  Beneficiary #4 _____

Annuity #3

 □ YES

 □ NO

- Type
   □ Fixed
   □ Variable
   □ Other _____
- Owner of Annuity _____
- Name of Insurer _____
- Place of Purchase _____
- Name of Agent _____
- Address _____
- City _____ State _____ Zip _____
- Phone _____ Fax _____ Cell _____
- E-mail _____
- Contract # _____
- Value (approximately) _____
- Beneficiary (Name, Address, Phone(s), Fax, Cell, E-mail)
   Beneficiary #1 _____
   Beneficiary #2 _____
   Beneficiary #3 _____
   Beneficiary #4 _____

SOCIAL SECURITY AND VETERAN'S PLAN

☐ YES
☐ NO

☐ Social Security
☐ U.S. Military Veteran's Plan

Note: Contact Social Security Administration for death benefits and timetable for claiming death benefits.

Social Security Administration Office of Public Inquiries
Windsor Park Building
6401 Security Blvd. Baltimore, MD 21235
1(800) 772-1213
www.ssa.gov

_____
_____
_____
_____
_____
_____
_____
_____
_____
_____
_____
_____
_____
_____
_____
_____
_____

STOCKS AND BONDS AND OTHER INVESTMENTS

Firm Name #1 _____
- ☐ YES
- ☐ NO
- Address _____
- City _____ State _____ Zip _____
- Branch _____
- Contact Person _____
- Phone _____ Fax _____ Cell _____
- E-mail _____
- Account #1

  Account # _____

  Account Title _____
- Account #2

  Account # _____

  Account Title _____
- Account #3

  Account # _____

  Account Title _____
- Account #4

  Account # _____

  Account Title _____

Firm Name #2 _____

    ☐ YES

    ☐ NO

- Address _____
- City _____ State _____ Zip _____
- Branch _____
- Contact Person _____
- Phone _____ Fax _____ Cell _____
- E-mail _____
- Account #1

    Account # _____

    Account Title _____

- Account #2

    Account # _____

    Account Title _____

- Account #3

    Account # _____

    Account Title _____

- Account #4

    Account # _____

    Account Title _____

BUSINESS OWNERSHIP

Business #1

☐ YES

☐ NO

- Name of Business _____
- Address _____
- City _____ State _____ Zip _____
- Contact Person _____
- Phone _____ Fax _____ Cell _____
- E-mail _____

TYPE

☐ Manufacturing

☐ Sales

☐ Farming

☐ Other _____

- Debt Owed (Amount) _____
- Debt Paid (Date) _____
- Net Value (Approximately) _____

STRUCTURE

☐ Sole Ownership

☐ Partnership

Name of Partner(s) _____

Address _____

City _____ State _____ Zip _____

Phone _____ Fax _____ Cell _____

Date of Partnership _____

Percentage (%) of Partnership _____

☐ Corporation

Name of Principal(s) _____

Date Incorporated _____

County, State _____

Location of Corporate Seal _____

Business #2

☐ YES

☐ NO

- Name of Business _____
- Address _____
- City _____ State _____ Zip _____
- Contact Person _____
- Phone _____ Fax _____ Cell _____
- E-mail _____

TYPE

☐ Manufacturing

☐ Sales

☐ Farming

☐ Other _____

- Debt Owed (Amount) _____
- Debt Paid (Date) _____
- Net Value (Approximately) _____

STRUCTURE

☐ Sole Ownership

☐ Partnership

Name of Partner(s) _____

Address _____

City _____ State _____ Zip _____

Phone _____ Fax _____ Cell _____

Date of Partnership _____

Percentage (%) of Partnership _____

☐ Corporation

Name of Principal(s) _____

Date Incorporated _____

County, State _____

Location of Corporate Seal _____

COMMENTS _____

_____

_____

_____

_____

_____

_____

_____

_____

_____

_____

_____

_____

_____

_____

_____

_____

_____

_____

CHAPTER FIVE

LEGAL:
DOT THE I'S & CROSS THE T'S

CHAPTER FIVE

LEGAL:
DOT THE I'S AND CROSS THE T'S

Taking care of legalities is not only a pain in the neck, it's a pain in the pocketbook. Nevertheless, dealing with legal matters is a necessity. The more you take care of this before you die, the easier it can be for your heirs after you die.

We hear of so many people who have never made a Will or who haven't updated it in the last 20 years. If you have a Will, update it regularly. Depending on the total value of everything you have, an alternative to a Will might be to put your home, car and personal belongings in a Trust, possibly saving the cost and time of probate. Either way, get legal advice from an attorney and start your planning now. It is a good idea to also review who the beneficiary is on all your legal documents and accounts.

In this chapter you should list the particulars of your Will and Trusts, as well as all other relevant legal details, including whether you have a Uniform Donor Card or Living Will or Advance Health Care Directive.

LAWYER

- ☐ YES
- ☐ NO
- Name _____
- Name of Firm _____
- Address _____
- City _____ State _____ Zip _____
- Contact Person _____
- Phone _____ Fax _____ Cell _____
- E-mail _____

WILL

☐ YES

☐ NO

- Location _____
- Date of Document _____
- Date of Revisions _____
- Witnessed By _____
- Prepared by _____
- Address _____
- City _____ State _____ Zip _____

LIVING WILLS / HEALTH CARE / POWERS OF ATTORNEY / ADVANCE HEALTH CARE DIRECTIVES

☐ YES

☐ NO

- Date of Document _____
- Date of Revisions _____
- Location _____

TRUSTS

Trust #1

☐ YES

☐ NO

- Type of Trust _____
- Title of Trust _____
- Date of Document _____
- Date of Amendment(s) _____
- Location _____

Trust #2

☐ YES

☐ NO

- Type of Trust _____
- Title of Trust _____
- Date of Document _____
- Date of Amendment(s) _____
- Location _____

Trust #3

☐ YES

☐ NO

- Type of Trust _____
- Title of Trust _____
- Date of Document _____
- Date of Amendment(s) _____
- Location _____

POWER OF ATTORNEY

☐ YES
☐ NO

- Name / Person with Power of Attorney _____
- Name of Firm _____
- Address _____
- City _____ State _____ Zip _____
- Contact Person _____
- Phone _____ Fax _____ Cell _____
- E-mail _____
- Location _____

EXECUTOR OF WILL OR TRUSTEE

☐ YES
☐ NO

- Name _____
- Name of Company _____
- Address _____
- City _____ State _____ Zip _____
- Contact Person _____
- Phone _____ Fax _____ Cell _____
- E-mail _____
- Location _____

CHAPTER SIX

INSURANCE: GOT YOU COVERED

Chapter Six

Insurance:
Got You Covered

It is important to let your heirs know what policies you own and where to find them. Are they in a file or stored under the bed? This information can be critical if you have a car accident or the sudden need for long term care. Also, be sure to review the beneficiaries and the death benefits of your insurance policies.

In this chapter, you should write down the name of the insurance company, policy numbers, agent names, phone numbers and a brief description of each policy. This will save your heirs time and trouble. If you don't, there might be a delay in needed coverage or policies might lapse in your unforeseen absence.

Remember all these details are needed in an emergency. Keeping an extra copy of this book, away from your house, could save critical time, energy, and conflict.

LIFE INSURANCE

☐ YES
☐ NO

- Type
  ☐ Whole Life Insurance
  ☐ Universal Whole Life
  ☐ Term Insurance
  ☐ Variable Whole Life
  ☐ Variable Universal Life
  ☐ Double Indemnity
  ☐ Other _____

Life Insurance Policy #1

☐ YES
☐ NO

- Name of Policy Holder _____
- Policy # _____
- Face Value _____
- Type of Insurance _____
- Name of Insurer _____
- Place of Purchase _____
- Name of Agent _____
- Address _____
- City _____ State _____ Zip _____
- Phone _____ Fax _____ Cell _____
- E-mail _____
- Beneficiary (Name, Address, Phone(s), E-mail)
  Beneficiary #1 _____
  Beneficiary #2 _____

Life Insurance Policy #2

    ☐ YES

    ☐ NO

- Name of Policy Holder _____
- Policy # _____
- Face Value _____
- Type of Insurance _____
- Name of Insurer _____
- Place of Purchase _____
- Name of Agent _____
- Address _____
- City _____ State _____ Zip _____
- Phone _____ Fax _____ Cell _____
- E-mail _____
- Beneficiary (Name, Address, Phone(s), E-mail)
  Beneficiary #1 _____
  Beneficiary #2 _____

VEHICLE INSURANCE

- ☐ YES
- ☐ NO
- Type
  - ☐ Automobiles
  - ☐ Motorcycles
  - ☐ Boats
  - ☐ Planes
  - ☐ RV's
  - ☐ Other

Automobiles

- ☐ YES
- ☐ NO
- Name of Insurance Company _____
- Name of Agent _____
- Address _____
- City _____ State _____ Zip _____
- Phone _____ Fax _____ Cell _____
- E-mail _____
- Policy # _____
- VIN # _____
- License Plate # _____
- Year / Model _____
- Location of Vehicle _____
- Address _____
- City _____ State _____ Zip _____

Motorcycles

☐ YES

☐ NO

- Name of Insurance Company _____
- Name of Agent _____
- Address _____
- City _____ State _____ Zip _____
- Phone _____ Fax _____ Cell _____
- E-mail _____
- Policy # _____
- VIN # _____
- License Plate # _____
- Year / Model _____
- Location of Vehicle _____

Boats

☐ YES

☐ NO

- Name of Insurance Company _____
- Name of Agent _____
- Address _____
- City _____ State _____ Zip _____
- Phone _____ Fax _____ Cell _____
- E-mail _____
- Policy # _____
- VIN # _____
- License Plate # _____
- Year / Model _____
- Location of Boat _____

Planes

☐ YES

☐ NO

- Name of Insurance Company _____
- Name of Agent _____
- Address _____
- City _____ State _____ Zip _____
- Phone _____ Fax _____ Cell _____
- E-mail _____
- Policy # _____
- VIN # _____
- License Plate # _____
- Year / Model _____
- Location of Plane _____

RV's

☐ YES

☐ NO

- Name of Insurance Company _____
- Name of Agent _____
- Address _____
- City _____ State _____ Zip _____
- Phone _____ Fax _____ Cell _____
- E-mail _____
- Policy # _____
- VIN # _____
- License Plate # _____
- Year / Model _____
- Location of Vehicle _____

Other – Vehicle .

- ☐ YES
- ☐ NO
- Name of Insurance Company _____
- Name of Agent _____
- Address _____
- City _____ State _____ Zip _____
- Phone _____ Fax _____ Cell _____
- E-mail _____
- Policy # _____
- VIN # _____
- License Plate # _____
- Year / Model _____
- Location of Vehicle _____

HOME INSURANCE

- ☐ YES
- ☐ NO
- Types
  - ☐ Homeowners
  - ☐ Fire
  - ☐ Flood
  - ☐ Earthquake
  - ☐ Hurricane
  - ☐ Tornado
  - ☐ Theft
  - ☐ Personal Liability
  - ☐ Other(s)

Homeowners

- ☐ YES
- ☐ NO
- Insurance Company _____
- Agency _____
- Name of Agent _____
- Address _____
- City _____ State _____ Zip _____
- Phone _____ Fax _____ Cell _____
- E-mail _____
- Policy # _____

Fire

☐ YES

☐ NO

- Insurance Company _____
- Agency _____
- Name of Agent _____
- Address _____
- City _____ State _____ Zip _____
- Phone _____ Fax _____ Cell _____
- E-mail _____
- Policy # _____

Flood

☐ YES

☐ NO

- Insurance Company _____
- Agency _____
- Name of Agent _____
- Address _____
- City _____ State _____ Zip _____
- Phone _____ Fax _____ Cell _____
- E-mail _____
- Policy # _____

Earthquake
- ☐ YES
- ☐ NO
- Insurance Company _____
- Agency _____
- Name of Agent _____
- Address _____
- City _____ State _____ Zip _____
- Phone _____ Fax _____ Cell _____
- E-mail _____
- Policy # _____

Hurricane
- ☐ YES
- ☐ NO
- Insurance Company _____
- Agency _____
- Name of Agent _____
- Address _____
- City _____ State _____ Zip _____
- Phone _____ Fax _____ Cell _____
- E-mail _____
- Policy # _____

Tornado

☐ YES

☐ NO

- Insurance Company _____
- Agency _____
- Name of Agent _____
- Address _____
- City _____ State _____ Zip _____
- Phone _____ Fax _____ Cell _____
- E-mail _____
- Policy # _____

Theft

☐ YES

☐ NO

- Insurance Company _____
- Agency _____
- Name of Agent _____
- Address _____
- City _____ State _____ Zip _____
- Phone _____ Fax _____ Cell _____
- E-mail _____
- Policy # _____

Personal Liability

☐ YES

☐ NO

- Insurance Company _____
- Agency _____
- Name of Agent _____
- Address _____
- City _____ State _____ Zip _____
- Phone _____ Fax _____ Cell _____
- E-mail _____
- Policy # _____

Other – Policy _____

☐ YES

☐ NO

- Insurance Company _____
- Agency _____
- Name of Agent _____
- Address _____
- City _____ State _____ Zip _____
- Phone _____ Fax _____ Cell _____
- E-mail _____
- Policy # _____

MEDICAL INSURANCE

- ☐ YES
- ☐ NO
- Type
  - ☐ Medical
  - ☐ Major Medical
  - ☐ Dental
  - ☐ Medicare / Medi-Cal / Medicaid
  - ☐ Vision
  - ☐ Hospitalization
  - ☐ Surgical
  - ☐ Worker's Disability and Compensation
  - ☐ Long Term Health Care
  - ☐ Pet
  - ☐ Other

Medical

- ☐ YES
- ☐ NO
- Insurance Company _____
- Agency _____
- Name of Agent _____
- Address _____
- City _____ State _____ Zip _____
- Phone _____ Fax _____ Cell _____
- E-mail _____
- Policy # _____
- ID # _____
- Contract Code # _____
- Other # _____

Major Medical

☐ YES

☐ NO

- Insurance Company _____
- Agency _____
- Name of Agent _____
- Address _____
- City _____ State _____ Zip _____
- Phone _____ Fax _____ Cell _____
- E-mail _____
- Policy # _____
- ID # _____
- Contract Code # _____
- Other # _____

Dental

☐ YES

☐ NO

- Insurance Company _____
- Agency _____
- Name of Agent _____
- Address _____
- City _____ State _____ Zip _____
- Phone _____ Fax _____ Cell _____
- E-mail _____
- Policy # _____
- ID # _____
- Contract Code # _____
- Other # _____

Medicare / Medi-Cal / Medicaid

☐ YES
☐ NO

- Insurance Company _____
- Agency _____
- Name of Agent _____
- Address _____
- City _____ State _____ Zip _____
- Phone _____ Fax _____ Cell _____
- E-mail _____
- Policy # _____
- ID # _____
- Contract Code # _____
- Other # _____
- Supplement _____

Vision

☐ YES
☐ NO

- Insurance Company _____
- Agency _____
- Name of Agent _____
- Address _____
- City _____ State _____ Zip _____
- Phone _____ Fax _____ Cell _____
- E-mail _____
- Policy # _____
- ID # _____
- Contract Code # _____
- Other # _____

Hospitalization

☐ YES

☐ NO

- Insurance Company _____
- Agency _____
- Name of Agent _____
- Address _____
- City _____ State _____ Zip _____
- Phone _____ Fax _____ Cell _____
- E-mail _____
- Policy # _____
- ID # _____
- Contract Code # _____
- Other # _____

Surgical

☐ YES

☐ NO

- Insurance Company _____
- Agency _____
- Name of Agent _____
- Address _____
- City _____ State _____ Zip _____
- Phone _____ Fax _____ Cell _____
- E-mail _____
- Policy # _____
- ID # _____
- Contract Code # _____
- Other # _____

Worker's Disability and Compensation
- ☐ YES
- ☐ NO
- Insurance Company _____
- Agency _____
- Name of Agent _____
- Address _____
- City _____ State _____ Zip _____
- Phone _____ Fax _____ Cell _____
- E-mail _____
- Policy # _____
- ID # _____
- Contract Code # _____
- Other # _____

Long Term Health Care
- ☐ YES
- ☐ NO
- Insurance Company _____
- Agency _____
- Name of Agent _____
- Address _____
- City _____ State _____ Zip _____
- Phone _____ Fax _____ Cell _____
- E-mail _____
- Policy # _____
- ID # _____
- Contract Code # _____
- Other # _____

Pet

    ☐ YES

    ☐ NO

- Insurance Company _____
- Agency _____
- Name of Agent _____
- Address _____
- City _____ State _____ Zip _____
- Phone _____ Fax _____ Cell _____
- E-mail _____
- Policy # _____
- ID # _____
- Contract Code # _____
- Other # _____

Other _____

    ☐ YES

    ☐ NO

- Insurance Company _____
- Agency _____
- Name of Agent _____
- Address _____
- City _____ State _____ Zip _____
- Phone _____ Fax _____ Cell _____
- E-mail _____
- Policy # _____
- ID # _____
- Contract Code # _____
- Other # _____

CHAPTER SEVEN

MEDICAL: FROM HEAD TO TOE

CHAPTER SEVEN

MEDICAL: FROM HEAD TO TOE

All information regarding your physical and mental health should be listed in this chapter.

It might not occur to you, but in case of an accident or sudden illness, your family and friends should know the names of your physicians, your current medications, your pharmacy, which hospitals you prefer, and if you have a legal document for someone to make medical decisions for you. Also, if you have Long Term Healthcare, it is listed under Insurance in Chapter Six.

Planning ahead in your life, may include thinking about what senior living options are available to you, besides your current home.

Visiting local facilities can give you some idea, of the type of care and cost involved, should you need it.

Talk it over with your family so that they know your priorities. Stay involved in the process. Otherwise, you might end up somewhere you do not want to be, simply because no one knew what you really wanted. Let your choices be known.

DOCTORS

- ☐ YES
- ☐ NO
- Type
  - ☐ Medical
  - ☐ Psychiatrist / Psychologist
  - ☐ Chiropractor
  - ☐ Physical Therapist
  - ☐ Homeopathic
  - ☐ Chinese Medicine
  - ☐ Integrated/ Alternative
  - ☐ Health Practitioner
  - ☐ Pet
  - ☐ Other

Medical Doctor #1
- ☐ YES
- ☐ NO
- Specialty _____
- Name _____
- Address _____
- City _____ State _____ Zip _____
- Phone _____ Fax _____ Cell _____
- E-mail _____

Medical Doctor #2

- ☐ YES
- ☐ NO
- Specialty _____
- Name _____
- Address _____
- City _____ State _____ Zip _____
- Phone _____ Fax _____ Cell _____
- E-mail _____

Medical Doctor #3

- ☐ YES
- ☐ NO
- Specialty _____
- Name _____
- Address _____
- City _____ State _____ Zip _____
- Phone _____ Fax _____ Cell _____
- E-mail _____

Medical Doctor #4

- ☐ YES
- ☐ NO
- Specialty _____
- Name _____
- Address _____
- City _____ State _____ Zip _____
- Phone _____ Fax _____ Cell _____
- E-mail _____

Psychiatrist / Psychologist #1

☐ YES

☐ NO

- Specialty _____
- Name _____
- Address _____
- City _____ State _____ Zip _____
- Phone _____ Fax _____ Cell _____
- E-mail _____

Psychiatrist / Psychologist #2

☐ YES

☐ NO

- Specialty _____
- Name _____
- Address _____
- City _____ State _____ Zip _____
- Phone _____ Fax _____ Cell _____
- E-mail _____

Chiropractor

☐ YES

☐ NO

- Specialty _____
- Name _____
- Address _____
- City _____ State _____ Zip _____
- Phone _____ Fax _____ Cell _____
- E-mail _____

Physical Therapist

- ☐ YES
- ☐ NO
- Specialty _____
- Name _____
- Address _____
- City _____ State _____ Zip _____
- Phone _____ Fax _____ Cell _____
- E-mail _____

Homeopathic Practitioner

- ☐ YES
- ☐ NO
- Specialty _____
- Name _____
- Address _____
- City _____ State _____ Zip _____
- Phone _____ Fax _____ Cell _____
- E-mail _____

Chinese Medicine

- ☐ YES
- ☐ NO
- Specialty _____
- Name _____
- Address _____
- City _____ State _____ Zip _____
- Phone _____ Fax _____ Cell _____
- E-mail _____

Integrated / Alternative #1

- ☐ YES
- ☐ NO
- Specialty _____
- Name _____
- Address _____
- City _____ State _____ Zip _____
- Phone _____ Fax _____ Cell _____
- E-mail _____

Integrated / Alternative #2

- ☐ YES
- ☐ NO
- Specialty _____
- Name _____
- Address _____
- City _____ State _____ Zip _____
- Phone _____ Fax _____ Cell _____
- E-mail _____

Health Practitioner #1

- ☐ YES
- ☐ NO
- Specialty _____
- Name _____
- Address _____
- City _____ State _____ Zip _____
- Phone _____ Fax _____ Cell _____
- E-mail _____

Health Practitioner #2

    ☐ YES

    ☐ NO

- Specialty _____
- Name _____
- Address _____
- City _____ State _____ Zip _____
- Phone _____ Fax _____ Cell _____
- E-mail _____

DENTISTS

    ☐ YES

    ☐ NO

Dentist

- Specialty _____
- Name _____
- Address _____
- City _____ State _____ Zip _____
- Phone _____ Fax _____ Cell _____
- E-mail _____

PHARMACY

☐ YES
☐ NO

- Name _____
- Address _____
- City _____ State _____ Zip _____
- Phone _____ Fax _____ Cell _____
- E-mail _____
- Website _____
- Username _____
- Password _____

- Name _____
- Address _____
- City _____ State _____ Zip _____
- Phone _____ Fax _____ Cell _____
- E-mail _____
- Website _____
- Username _____
- Password _____

CURRENT PRESCRIPTIONS AND DOSAGES

☐ YES
☐ NO

Date	Medication Name	Dosage / Day	Prescribed by

HOSPITAL

Hospital (First Choice)

- ☐ YES
- ☐ NO
- Name _____
- Address _____
- City _____ State _____ Zip _____
- Contact Person _____
- Phone _____ Fax _____ Cell _____
- E-mail _____
- Website _____

Hospital (Second Choice)

- ☐ YES
- ☐ NO
- Name _____
- Address _____
- City _____ State _____ Zip _____
- Contact Person _____
- Phone _____ Fax _____ Cell _____
- E-mail _____
- Website _____

PROVIDING SENIOR CARE LIVING

☐ YES

☐ NO

- Type
  - ☐ Independent Living
  - ☐ Assisted Living
  - ☐ Rehabilitation
  - ☐ In-Home Care
  - ☐ Long Term Health Care
  - ☐ Hospice
  - ☐ Other

Independent Living

☐ YES

☐ NO

- Name _____
- Address _____
- City _____ State _____ Zip _____
- Contact Person _____
- Phone _____ Fax _____ Cell _____
- E-mail _____
- Website _____

Assisted Living

☐ YES

☐ NO

- Name _____
- Address _____
- City _____ State _____ Zip _____
- Contact Person _____
- Phone _____ Fax _____ Cell _____
- E-mail _____
- Website _____

Rehabilitation

☐ YES

☐ NO

- Name _____
- Address _____
- City _____ State _____ Zip _____
- Contact Person _____
- Phone _____ Fax _____ Cell _____
- E-mail _____
- Website _____

In-Home Care

    ☐ YES

    ☐ NO

- Name _____
- Address _____
- City _____ State _____ Zip _____
- Contact Person _____
- Phone _____ Fax _____ Cell _____
- E-mail _____
- Website _____

Long Term Health Care

    ☐ YES

    ☐ NO

- Name _____
- Address _____
- City _____ State _____ Zip _____
- Contact Person _____
- Phone _____ Fax _____ Cell _____
- E-mail _____
- Website _____

Hospice

    ☐ YES

    ☐ NO

- Name _____
- Address _____
- City _____ State _____ Zip _____
- Contact Person _____
- Phone _____ Fax _____ Cell _____
- E-mail _____
- Website _____

Other – Type of Care _____

    ☐ YES

    ☐ NO

- Name _____
- Address _____
- City _____ State _____ Zip _____
- Contact Person _____
- Phone _____ Fax _____ Cell _____
- E-mail _____
- Website _____

VETERINARIAN

☐ YES
☐ NO

- Name _____
- Address _____
- City _____ State _____ Zip _____
- Contact Person _____
- Phone _____ Fax _____ Cell _____
- E-mail _____
- Website _____

- Name _____
- Address _____
- City _____ State _____ Zip _____
- Contact Person _____
- Phone _____ Fax _____ Cell _____
- E-mail _____
- Website _____

CHAPTER EIGHT

FUNERALS: THE LAST HURRAH

CHAPTER EIGHT

FUNERALS:
THE LAST HURRAH

This is it. The End. The Last Hurrah.

Now is your chance to do your family and friends a huge favor. Write down your last wishes. They will sing praises to your name because they do not have to guess at what you want done. Do you want a quiet family only funeral or a wild and crazy party? Indoors or outdoors? Religious or nonreligious?

It isn't a subject comfortable for us to face, but it's an important one. It also might not seem like a big deal until you are the one making all these decisions for someone else. It is, in fact, a huge responsibility. You know yourself best. What do you want? Once you get into the swing of it, you might even get a kick out of thinking about all the ways you can wave good-bye.

When you complete this chapter, you can close the book knowing that your last wishes will be carried out as desired. You have eased the burden on those that will benefit from your invaluable gift, your "Legacy."

CHECK LIST FOR ORGANIZING
AND PLANNING A FUNERAL

A funeral may require many people working together to handle to the various jobs. The person in charge of each job has been given the title of "Organizer" and is listed next to each category. This will help you keep track of who is doing what. Copies of these pages should be given to all "Organizers."

FUNERAL

Organizer Name _____

Phone _____ Fax _____ Cell _____

E-mail _____ Job Completed ☐

Funeral Home

☐ YES

☐ NO

- Name _____
- Address _____
- City _____ State _____ Zip _____
- Contact Person _____
- Phone _____ Fax _____ Cell _____
- E-mail _____
- Comments _____

_____

_____

_____

_____

_____

_____

_____

_____

Funeral Insurance Policy
- ☐ YES
- ☐ NO
- Policy # _____
- Name _____
- Address _____
- City _____ State _____ Zip _____
- Phone _____ Fax _____ Cell _____
- E-mail _____
- Comments _____
- _____
- _____

Rest Home / Hospice Agreements
- ☐ YES
- ☐ NO
- Contracts To Be Canceled or Refunded _____

Disposition of Remains
- ☐ Earth Burial
- ☐ Cremation
- ☐ No Embalming
- ☐ Neptune Society
- ☐ Entombment / Mausoleum
- ☐ Immediate Burial – No Viewing
- ☐ Heir's Decision
- ☐ Other _____

Donor Card

- ☐ YES
- ☐ NO

- Location _____
- Address _____
- City _____ State _____ Zip _____

Religious Preference

- ☐ YES
- ☐ NO
- ☐ Catholic
- ☐ Protestant
- ☐ Jewish
- ☐ Muslim
- ☐ Buddhist
- ☐ Hindu
- ☐ Other _____

Religious Institution

- ☐ YES
- ☐ NO

- Name _____
- Address _____
- City _____ State _____ Zip _____
- Phone _____ Fax _____ Cell _____
- E-mail _____
- Comments _____

_____
_____
_____
_____
_____
_____
_____
_____

FUNERAL SERVICE LOCATION

Organizer Name _____

Phone _____ Fax _____ Cell _____

E-mail _____ Job Completed ☐

- ☐ Funeral Home
- ☐ Residence
- ☐ House of Worship
- ☐ Gravesite
- ☐ Memorial Society Membership
- ☐ Other

- Name _____
- Address _____
- City _____ State _____ Zip _____
- Contact Person _____
- Phone _____ Fax _____ Cell _____
- E-mail _____
- Map / Reception Directions _____

_____
_____
_____
_____

Funeral Service Preference
- ☐ None
- ☐ Body Present
- ☐ Pallbearers _____
- ☐ Body Not Present
- ☐ Open Casket
- ☐ Closed Casket
- ☐ Type of Casket _____

GRAVESITE SERVICE

Organizer Name _____

Phone _____ Fax _____ Cell _____

E-mail _____ Job Completed ☐

☐ Private – Family Only
☐ Family and Friends
☐ Open to the Public
☐ To Be Decided by Family Members

☐ Reserve Seats for Family
☐ Music Preferred (taps, bagpipes, etc.) _____
_____

☐ Songs _____
_____

☐ Soloist(s) _____
☐ Preferred Hymn(s) _____
_____

☐ Readings / Poems, etc. _____
_____

☐ Favorite Flowers _____
☐ Choice of Clergy _____
☐ Eulogy Speakers _____
_____

☐ Clothes for My Burial _____
☐ Pallbearers _____
☐ Special Request _____
_____

Comments _____
_____
_____

Cemetery

Organizer Name _____
Phone _____ Fax _____ Cell _____
E-mail _____ Job Completed ☐

- Name _____
- Address _____
- City _____ State _____ Zip _____
- Contact Person _____
- Phone _____ Fax _____ Cell _____
- E-mail _____

Deed for Cemetery Plot
  ☐ YES
  ☐ NO
- Location of Deed _____
- Location of Plot and # _____

Headstone / Grave Marker

Organizer Name _____

Phone _____ Fax _____ Cell _____

E-mail _____ Job Completed ☐

- Material
  - ☐ Granite: Color _____
  - ☐ Marble: Color _____
  - ☐ Bronze
  - ☐ Veteran's
  - ☐ Other _____
- Symbols (flowers, birds, musical, etc.) _____
  _____
- Suggested Inscription _____
  _____
- Comments _____
  _____

MEMORIAL SERVICE

Organizer Name _____

Phone _____ Fax _____ Cell _____

E-mail _____ Job Completed ☐

☐ Private – Family Only

☐ Family and Friends

☐ Open to the Public

☐ To Be Decided by Family Members

☐ Reserve Seats for Family

☐ Location _____

☐ Music Preferred _____

_____

☐ Hymns / Songs _____

_____

☐ Organist _____

☐ Soloist(s) _____

☐ Eulogy Speakers _____

☐ Readings / Poems, etc. _____

_____

☐ Favorite Flowers _____

☐ Pallbearers _____

☐ Choice of Clergy _____

☐ Clothes for My Burial _____

☐ Special Request(s) _____

_____

_____

_____

_____

_____

_____

RECEPTION

Organizer Name _____

Phone _____ Fax _____ Cell _____

E-mail _____ Job Completed ☐

- Name _____
- Address _____
- City _____ State _____ Zip _____
- Phone _____ Fax _____ Cell _____
- E-mail _____
- Location of Reception _____
- Hours of Reception _____
  - ☐ Map with directions and phone # _____

  _____

  - ☐ Approximate # of Guests _____
  - ☐ Coordinator / Greeter (in case Hostess is not present when guests arrive)

  _____

  - ☐ Caterer _____
  - ☐ Pot Luck _____
  - ☐ Hors d'oeuvres / Buffet Table _____

  _____

  - ☐ Salads and side dishes _____

  _____

  - ☐ Sandwiches / Main Course _____

  _____

  _____

  _____

  _____

  _____

  _____

☐ Desserts _____
_____

☐ Beverages (coffee, tea, sodas, alcohol, ice)_____
☐ Bartenders _____
☐ Kitchen Helpers _____
☐ Servers _____
☐ Set Up Helpers _____
☐ Clean Up Helpers _____
☐ Flowers _____
☐ Dishes, Glasses, Dinner / Cocktail Napkins, Flatware _____
_____

☐ Tables, Chairs, Coat Racks, Trash Cans _____
_____

☐ Heaters, Awnings, Tents, Outside Lighting _____
☐ Valet Parking (company, hours of service, Cost per hour, # of valets) ___
_____

☐ Baby Sitters During Reception _____
☐ Music _____
☐ Photographs of Deceased _____
_____
_____
_____
_____
_____
_____
_____
_____
_____
_____
_____
_____
_____
_____

☐ Memorial Video _____

☐ Display Easels / Tables / Video Screen _____

_____

☐ Guest Book and Pens _____

☐ Location of Guest Book _____

☐ Hotel Accommodations for Out-of-Town Guests _____

_____

☐ Airline Reservations for Out-of-Town Guests _____

_____

☐ Transportation for Out-of Town Guests _____

_____

☐ Plan(s) for the Next Day _____

_____

☐ Meal(s) for the Next Day _____

NOTICE TO NEWSPAPERS, ORGANIZATIONS, ETC.

Organizer Name _____

Phone _____ Fax _____ Cell _____

E-mail _____ Job Completed ☐

Newspaper (Local)

☐ YES

☐ NO

- Name _____
- Address _____
- City _____ State _____ Zip _____
- Contact Person _____
- Phone _____ Fax _____ Cell _____
- E-mail _____

Newspaper (Out of State)

☐ YES

☐ NO

- Name _____
- Address _____
- City _____ State _____ Zip _____
- Contact Person _____
- Phone _____ Fax _____ Cell _____
- E-mail _____

Church

☐ YES

☐ NO

- Name _____
- Address _____
- City _____ State _____ Zip _____
- Contact Person _____
- Phone _____ Fax _____ Cell _____
- E-mail _____

Club

☐ YES

☐ NO

- Name _____
- Address _____
- City _____ State _____ Zip _____
- Contact Person _____
- Phone _____ Fax _____ Cell _____
- E-mail _____

Organizations

☐ YES

☐ NO

- Name _____
- Address _____
- City _____ State _____ Zip _____
- Contact Person _____
- Phone _____ Fax _____ Cell _____
- E-mail _____

High-School Alumni

☐ YES

☐ NO

- Name _____
- Address _____
- City _____ State _____ Zip _____
- Contact Person _____
- Phone _____ Fax _____ Cell _____
- E-mail _____

College Alumni

☐ YES

☐ NO

- Name _____
- Address _____
- City _____ State _____ Zip _____
- Contact Person _____
- Phone _____ Fax _____ Cell _____
- E-mail _____

Military Branch

☐ YES

☐ NO

- Name _____
- Address _____
- City _____ State _____ Zip _____
- Contact Person _____
- Phone _____ Fax _____ Cell _____
- E-mail _____

Professional Groups

☐ YES

☐ NO

- Name _____
- Address _____
- City _____ State _____ Zip _____
- Contact Person _____
- Phone _____ Fax _____ Cell _____
- E-mail _____

- Name _____
- Address _____
- City _____ State _____ Zip _____
- Contact Person _____
- Phone _____ Fax _____ Cell _____
- E-mail _____

- Name _____
- Address _____
- City _____ State _____ Zip _____
- Contact Person _____
- Phone _____ Fax _____ Cell _____
- E-mail _____

- Name _____
- Address _____
- City _____ State _____ Zip _____
- Contact Person _____
- Phone _____ Fax _____ Cell _____
- E-mail _____

OBITUARY

Organizer Name _____

Phone _____ Fax _____ Cell _____

E-mail _____ Job Completed ☐

    ☐ YES

    ☐ NO

I have written my Own Obituary

    ☐ YES

    ☐ NO

• Location of document _____

Possible Items to Cover in Obituary

    ☐ Notify Newspaper – Local / Out-of-State

    ☐ Date and Cause of Death _____

    ☐ Date and Place of Birth _____

    ☐ Parent(s) Name(s) _____

    ☐ Education _____

    ☐ Photo To Be Included (Description and Location of Photo) _____

    _____

    _____

    ☐ Occupation / Profession _____

    ☐ Title(s)_____

    _____

    ☐ Social / Fraternal Organizations _____

    _____

    ☐ Service Membership _____

- ☐ Unions _____
- ☐ Accomplishments of Merit / Awards _____
- ☐ _____
- ☐ Predeceased Family _____
- ☐ Charity Donations (in lieu of flowers) _____
- ☐ _____
- ☐ _____
- ☐ _____

- Comments _____

_____

_____

_____

_____

_____

_____

_____

_____

_____

_____

_____

_____

_____

_____

_____

_____

_____

_____

_____

_____

_____

_____

_____

_____

DEATH CERTIFICATES

Organizer Name _____

Phone _____ Fax _____ Cell _____

E-mail _____ Job Completed ☐

☐ YES
☐ NO

☐ How Many _____
☐ Send To _____
☐ All Financial Institutions (such as banks, loans, credit cards, brokerages)
☐ Federal, State, and Local Government
☐ Attorney
☐ Accountant
☐ Utilities
☐ Other _____

_____
_____
_____
_____
_____
_____
_____
_____
_____
_____
_____
_____
_____
_____
_____

FOLLOW UP

Organizer Name _____

Phone _____ Fax _____ Cell _____

E-mail _____ Job Completed ☐

Checklist for Days Ahead

☐ Thank You Notes _____

☐ House Maintenance (Name, Address, Phone #) _____
_____
_____

☐ Garden Maintenance (Name, Address, Phone #) _____
_____
_____

☐ House Cleaning (Name, Address, Phone #) _____
_____
_____

☐ Paying Bills (Name, Address, Phone #) _____
_____
_____

☐ Mail Picked Up / Continue Home Delivery (Name, Address, Phone #) _____
_____
_____

☐ Animal care _____

☐ Children / Schools _____

☐ Business Issues _____
_____
_____

☐ Accounting Issues _____
_____
_____

☐ Medical Costs – Hospital / Hospice / Rest Home _____
_____
_____

☐ Insurance / Personal / Property _____

_____

_____

☐ Real Estate Issues _____

_____

_____

☐ Donation of Clothing / Furniture _____

_____

_____

☐ Yard / Garage Sale _____

_____

_____

☐ Sale of Vehicles _____

• Comments _____

_____

_____

_____

_____

_____

_____

_____

_____

_____

_____

_____

_____

_____

_____

_____

_____

_____

CONTACT LIST

Name	Phone Cell	Notified of Death	Funeral Invite	Thank You
Address	Relationship			

Name	Phone Cell	Notified of Death	Funeral Invite	Thank You
Address	Relationship			

Name	Phone Cell	Notified of Death	Funeral Invite	Thank You
Address	Relationship			

Name	Phone Cell	Notified of Death	Funeral Invite	Thank You
Address	Relationship			

Name	Phone Cell	Notified of Death	Funeral Invite	Thank You
Address	Relationship			

Name	Phone Cell	Notified of Death	Funeral Invite	Thank You
Address	Relationship			

Name	Phone Cell	Notified of Death	Funeral Invite	Thank You
Address	Relationship			

Name	Phone Cell	Notified of Death	Funeral Invite	Thank You
Address	Relationship			

Name	Phone Cell	Notified of Death	Funeral Invite	Thank You
Address	Relationship			

Name	Phone Cell	Notified of Death	Funeral Invite	Thank You
Address	Relationship			

Name	Phone Cell	Notified of Death	Funeral Invite	Thank You
Address	Relationship			

Name	Phone Cell	Notified of Death	Funeral Invite	Thank You
Address	Relationship			

Name	Phone Cell	Notified of Death	Funeral Invite	Thank You
Address	Relationship			

Name	Phone Cell	Notified of Death	Funeral Invite	Thank You
Address	Relationship			

Name	Phone Cell	Notified of Death	Funeral Invite	Thank You
Address	Relationship			

Name	Phone Cell	Notified of Death	Funeral Invite	Thank You
Address	Relationship			

Name	Phone Cell	Notified of Death	Funeral Invite	Thank You
Address	Relationship			

Name	Phone Cell	Notified of Death	Funeral Invite	Thank You
Address	Relationship			

Name	Phone Cell	Notified of Death	Funeral Invite	Thank You
Address	Relationship			

Name	Phone Cell	Notified of Death	Funeral Invite	Thank You
Address	Relationship			

Name	Phone Cell	Notified of Death	Funeral Invite	Thank You
Address	Relationship			

Name	Phone Cell	Notified of Death	Funeral Invite	Thank You
Address	Relationship			

Name	Phone Cell	Notified of Death	Funeral Invite	Thank You
Address	Relationship			

NOTES

NOTES

NOTES

CPSIA information can be obtained at www.ICGtesting.com
Printed in the USA
BVOW051857211211

278954BV00001B/15/P